My Book of
Numbers

illustrated by Michael Garton

WINDMILL
BOOKS

1 comfy bed

one

What color is the pillow?

2 Can you find?  1 lamp    1 clock

2 teddy bears
two

1 ball

2 books

2 pictures

3

3 racing go-karts
three

4 Can you find? 3 balloons 1 spiral slide

4 carousel horses

four

What color is the tasty cotton candy?

3 basketballs

4 tents

4 flags

5 party hats

five

I'm going to eat a cupcake!

6 Can you find? 5 candles 5 drinks

7 inner tubes

seven

How many pink swim caps can you see?

8 Can you find? 1 lifeguard 7 floats

8 happy swimmers

eight

4 flip flops   5 towels   8 water wings   9

9 activity books

nine

What shape is the clock on the wall?

Everyone needs a paintbrush!

WOOF!

1 2 3 4 5
6 7 8 9 10

Can you find? 1 teacher 10 paintbrushes

10 excited children

ten

MEOW!

a

9 pencils

6 lunch boxes

WOOF!

4 posters

12 clucking chickens

twelve

4 mice   5 haystacks   3 cows

13

14 fluttery butterflies

fourteen

5 lily pads   6 flowers   4 bees

15

15 yellow bananas
fifteen

Can you find? 9 apples   5 peppers

16

16 sixteen crunchy carrots

What color are the juicy apples?

2 shopping carts

8 cherries

3 pineapples

18 pretty flowers

eighteen

How many white flowers can you see?

4 clouds   3 trees   1 dog

19

19 waving flags
nineteen

How many red flags can you find?

20 Can you find?

 1 ice cream

 2 children

20 pink seashells
twenty

3 starfish   4 gulls   5 crabs

1 2 3 4 5 6 7 8 9 10 11 12
13 14 15 16 17 18 19 20
21 22 23 24 25 26 27 28 29
30 31 32 33 34 35 36 37
38 39 40 41 42 43 44 45
46 47 48 49 50 51 52 53

54 55 56 57 58 59 60 61
62 63 64 65 66 67 68 69
70 71 72 73 74 75 76 77
78 79 80 81 82 83 84 85
86 87 88 89 90 91 92 93
94 95 96 97 98 99 100

Can you find?

Look back in your book to see if you can find the following things.

plane

cake

ball

clock

horse

basket

swings

bucket

Cataloging-in-Publication Data

Names: Garton, Michael, illustrator.
Title: Numbers / illustrated by Michael Garton.
Description: New York : Windmill Books, 2019. | Series: My book of

Identifiers: ISBN 9781508196525 (pbk.) | ISBN 9781508196518 (library bound) | ISBN 9781508196532 (6 pack)
Subjects: LCSH: Counting–Pictorial works–Juvenile literature. | Counting–Juvenile literature.
Classification: LCC QA113.G37 2019 | DDC 513.2′11–dc23

Manufactured in the United States of America

CPSIA Compliance Information: Batch BS18WM: For Further Information contact Rosen Publishing, New York, New York at 1-800-237-9932

For web resources related to the subject of this book, go to: www.windmillbooks.com/weblinks and select this book's title.